PRAISE FOR
FARM GIRL LEAVES HOME
BY MARGARET FLETCHER

"Fletcher is a marvel in word and spirit. Her honest account of how she remained alive and absolutely thrived in a world filled with sadness and pain is an inspiration to us all. Her story eloquently speaks of her courage to leave the strong pulls of family at the age of 16 to a destiny that unfolded with each miraculous turn. Her accomplishments are extraordinary and yet her narrative will resonate with all who have met and overcome adversity."

Robin Levien President, Power2 You Coaching

"Margaret Fletcher gives us a rare glimpse, in a flow-of-consciousness style of writing, into an incredible life of accomplishment while struggling with and conquering debilitating diseases—any one of which commonly destroy life and spirit. Never before have I read such a raw and unbridled release of personal truth and experiences, in such a public way, in an effort to share life's hard-found lessons. Margaret's 'solutions found' will undoubtedly be treasured by her granddaughter, Shana, and they are met with my admiration of her unselfish sharing, which should be instructive to us all. How many of us have wished that we thought to ask, or had the opportunity, to delve into the minds and experiences of our grandparents, mothers, fathers, aunts, or uncles after they have passed and we are not able. How lucky Shana is to have this book... and Margaret."

D. Reece Pierce President and Director of Continuing Medical Education Co.

"*Farm Girl Leaves Home* is a gripping American narrative, a book of inspiration and help to all of us who meet difficulties in life such as mental illness, addictions, incurable chronic illnesses, divorce, job loss, and even death. Many people facing these life problems are told nothing more can be done. When we are broken and desperate we might find that this is the best time to let remarkable healing, transformation and life happen. Even the darkest moments in our life can be gifts that help us grow. Wellness, love, and joy come from within and are always possible. You must read Dr. Margaret Fletcher's book. This is sooooo important!"

Dr. Neil Shulman Associate Professor at Emory University School of Medicine, healthcare activist, screenwriter, and director *(Doc Hollywood)*

FARM GIRL LEAVES HOME

BY MARGARET FLETCHER

COPYRIGHT

Copyright © Margaret Fletcher, 2015

All rights reserved. No part of this book may be reproduced in any form without permission in writing from the author. Reviewers may quote brief passages in reviews.

ISBN: 978-1-942646-60-0

Library of Congress Control Number: 2015958122

DISCLAIMER

No part of this publication may be reproduced or transmitted in any form or by any means, mechanical or electronic, including photocopying or recording, or by any information storage and retrieval system, or transmitted by email without permission in writing from the author.

Neither the author nor the publisher assumes any responsibility for errors, omissions, or contrary interpretations of the subject matter herein. Any perceived slight of any individual or organization is purely unintentional.

Brand and product names are trademarks or registered trademarks of their respective owners.

This book contains discussions about medical problems and health issues. The author has her own opinions based on her training, skill, experience, and knowledge. If you should have questions about a medical problem, please refer to your primary care physician or medical specialty consultant. Please be advised that the author cannot be held accountable for medical decisions you make as a result of reading this book. Please consult your physician before undertaking any recommendations the author may make.

Cover Design: John Matthews
Interior Design: Heidi Miller
Editing: Grace Kerina
Author's photo courtesy of John Matthews

DEDICATION

To Shana Lia Fletcher, who taught me joy and love

TABLE OF CONTENTS

1	INTRODUCTION	
4	**CHAPTER 1** Life Was Not All Well in Paradise	
18	**CHAPTER 2** Lucky Breaks	
36	**CHAPTER 3** Medical School / The Honeymoon's Over	
46	**CHAPTER 4** Like Mother, Like Daughter	
58	**CHAPTER 5** The Last Party	
74	ACKNOWLEDGMENTS	
76	ABOUT THE AUTHOR	

THE EVENING TRAIN

I see the soft orange glow of the setting sun.
I smell the soft wet spring green grass.
Mother had recently come home from the asylum.
She said, "Pack your bags, go to school.
You don't need to stay here."

I didn't say goodbye to Dad; he was mad and milking.
I didn't say goodbye to the kids; I was afraid.
One suitcase has all my clothes,
the other, sausage sandwiches, just in case.
My red dress is sister Pat's.

A long black shadow leads me down the road,
to the station.

I see the engine rounding the bend,
Cutting through the black trees.
The train is taking me away;
I have no home.

INTRODUCTION

This book was written as a love letter to my granddaughter Shana Fletcher. Shana is 17 years old and will be finishing high school in a year. She is the same age I was when I left home and started the process of letting go.

I am writing this for several reasons. Letting go of family ties and leaving home can be a difficult time for anyone. Our doubts about ourselves, our fears of the future, and worries about our family of origin can be overwhelming. As Shana goes through this time in her life (and always) I want her to know that I love her deeply and that her family loves her more than she can know at this time.

I also want her to know the truth of my story. The road I followed—college, career, marriage, and family—to avoid my own growing pains did not prevent pain and suffering in my life. Carl Jung, psychoanalyst, said "The greatest burden a child must bear is the unlived life of the parents." Much suffering in my life came from wishing that my life could be different from my family story. I hoped that I could help my mother. I tried, and it didn't work.

When Shana or any person is following his or her own truth, the whole universe will respond to help, and is joyful. Mistakes will be made, but no matter how dark they seem, there will be options to either change or to continue. When you are in a free fall and life feels like it is coming at you from all directions, stop for a moment, look around, let your own inner wisdom help, and then ask for help from others. The universe will respond, and you might fall into the loving arms of a totally unknown person who is there to catch you.

Life, with all of its joys and suffering, is our teacher.

CHAPTER 1

LIFE WAS NOT ALL WELL IN PARADISE

Dear Shana,

You already know a lot of this story, but I wanted to share it with you in this format so you will always have it with you. As you know, this is a part of your history and your legacy. Any strength you see in me in this story is yours to claim for yourself when you need it.

My home on the farm in Michigan, where I grew up, was located on Paradise Hill. This is a two-mile rise of land off the banks of Lake Superior. It was beautiful there. The winter night snow shone like diamonds with the moonlight and aurora borealis. Often we lay on the dewy grass in the summer looking at meteor showers in the sky, or we would catch bottles of fireflies after all the hay was in the barn, around eleven at night. The sun didn't really set until then.

When I was twelve, I often found my mother looking sad and curled up on the davenport. She wouldn't talk. I would pull up a stool and sit with her, reach for her hand, and she would push me away. I asked her what was wrong, and she would start to cry. I was sure I had done something wrong to cause her suffering.

Was it the fur collar I cut off her fur coat for my doll?

Was it because I lost her birthstone ring that had been in the sewing machine drawer?

I didn't know what was wrong.

Mother still went into the barn to milk every morning and evening, but it seemed that she was thinking of something. This often lasted for days, and then things would be quiet until the sadness came back. My job was mainly in the house, cooking for the family—and there were six of us kids then—or doing laundry, and also sewing clothes from feed sacks. These might seem like simple jobs, with today's appliances. My laundry day started early in the morning by filling copper boilers full of water and heating them on the wood stove that was fired up. We had a wringer, and tub for rinsing, and we hung the clothes outside. There they would freeze-dry on the barbed wire fence in the winter or air dry on the clothesline in the summer. I spent lots of time planting strawberries, weeding the mile-long rows, or helping with the haymaking and chickens.

When I was thirteen, my Aunt Ruth called and asked me to come to work at Broemer Dairy, making shakes, hamburgers, ice cream cones, and keeping customers happy. That was good for me, as I could get out of the house, see new people, and really laugh and have fun. Ruth was seven years older than me and was more like an older sister. She was my mother's youngest sister and the eleventh of twelve kids.

When there were no customers at Broemer's, we restocked the refrigerators with gallon bottles of milk, or played the jukebox and sang to songs like "How Much is that Doggie in the Window" and crazy Hank Williams love songs. The money I made, 25 cents an hour, helped a lot to buy clothes for my sister Sal and me. I also could save more than when I was only doing the seasonal work of picking potatoes and strawberries, and doing the babysitting jobs that kept us going and kept me dreaming of a different life.

WHEN I WAS fifteen we had a long winter. The cows and chickens had to be kept in the barn from the end of October to near the end of May. The chickens seemed to crave the knee-high grass instead of their usual corn. Soon it was clear that they were not eating, and they weren't laying eggs. Their necks were swollen as big as grapefruits because their gizzards were blocked with grass. I guess there were no stones in them to grind it up.

My Dad was mad. "Now we have to kill 200 chickens for stew." The money we got from selling eggs paid for our groceries. The rest of the farm's income went back into machinery and cow food. "Why can't we just cut open their necks and clear the gizzards out?" I asked. He threw up his arms and hissed and left to go to town.

I figured the chickens were ready for stew anyway, so why not try something? My sister Sally was my sidekick. She was seven years old and would help me. We gathered up a knife, darning needle, thread, and needle-nose pliers, along with my dad's whisky from the beam in the dark basement, and set it all up in the milk house. We were ready.

Sally held a chicken down by the head and feet, wings tucked underneath. We learned the whiskey was not needed, or even useful, after the first chicken. They were too starved to put up a fight. I made a four-inch incision across the middle of the chicken's neck. There were no feathers there because the skin was stretched and pink. I opened the gizzard and used the pliers to pull out the rotten, stinking grass. Using the pliers was hopelessly slow, so I just used my fingers. Then I closed the incision with an overhand locking stitch, just like I used when hemming a skirt. We operated on several chickens to see what would happen, then I put them in a box in the woodshed.

The next morning, I hated to open the woodshed door to see what had happened to those chickens. But when I did, the chickens flew up, trying to get out, and there was an egg in the box. My surgeries had been successful. Maybe now my dad wouldn't be so mad.

Operating on animals was not new to me. Every Saturday night I chopped the heads off two chickens so we could have chicken for dinner on Sunday.

Also, cows would get obstructed from eating the wrong food and have to be opened up to relieve the gas. But when I did the chickens, that was a new kind of animal operation—one I had invented myself. And it worked!

It was interesting that, fifteen years later, Sally came to live with my husband and me. At that time, she was training to be a scrub tech at the University of Michigan, while I was training to be a head and neck surgeon. I wondered how our early days playing doctor and assistant to those chickens had influenced our life choices.

MOTHER'S EPISODES of sadness continued. She would often start big projects, like scrubbing the walls in the kitchen and scrubbing the floors–a type of spring-cleaning. I helped, but we didn't talk much. One task that seemed to bring relaxation and solace to her was to burn the paper trash in the fire pit near the woodshed. Tending the fire seemed to be a type of meditation for her.

One morning, I woke up to find the house spotless, but Mother's overalls were bloody and folded on the stairs.

What had happened? She'd taken some bottles and cans to the dump, which was along the creek, and had fallen off the bridge into the dump. This scared me. How had it happened? Why?

I REMEMBER ONE winter night at the kitchen table when I was cleaning eggs, my brother Willie was drying them, and sister Pat was weighing them and packing them into boxes. Dad came in and said, "You have a new baby brother. His name is Tom." There was silence. Pregnancy wasn't an open subject at home. Seven years previously, I'd learned only from the kids at school that my mother was "expecting," shortly before my sister Sally was born. This time around, I'd seen that Mom was getting "fat." Nobody talked. We paused the egg cleaning for a few seconds, and then continued our work.

This was another one of those times when I felt much confusion. I wanted to know how we would manage. Had the pregnancy been causing the sadness? Was my dad happy? Were we supposed to be happy, fearful, or ashamed? Why couldn't we talk? What were we feeling? How was this going to work? How could I not have known? Mother's sadness had been there for many years. Would this new baby help? Or was it about to get worse?

When Mom came home from the hospital, she was still sad. A few days later, while washing diapers, she told me she was embarrassed to be so old having a baby while the other women in the hospital were so young. She was 43. Her own mother had been 45 when her twelfth and last child was born.

Mother's sadness became more aggressive after Tom was born. We couldn't predict what was going to happen. My dad became much more irritable, too. We were all going around looking at each other in our peripheral vision. Don't make any eye contact, someone might go crazy. We all walked on eggshells, afraid to talk. It became clear that at least one of us would need to stay awake at night to watch, to be sure Mom stayed in bed, hopefully sleeping– which didn't ever seem to happen.

One morning, Dad shouted up the stairs in the middle of the night, "Everyone get up, right away!"

We all ran down immediately, like firemen on call. No one had been sleeping well.

"Mom's gone. I don't know where!"

Her coat was there, and Mom didn't drive, so it seemed she'd left the house in her nightgown. It was 20 degrees below zero outside. Dad grabbed all the blankets off their bed, and Willie took the flashlights. They left with the toboggan and followed Mother's tracks in the snow, which led toward the woods a half-mile away. They found her huddled in a cave next to a steep red sandstone rock cliff. They'd wrapped her in the blankets and were coming back home with her already when the rest of us caught up to them.

She was blue, eyes staring ahead, and she seemed frozen all over. We took her to the hospital. When she'd warmed up, she could move again but her feet were purple, and the doctor was afraid she would lose at least the toes. They cared for her, and I stayed by her side—no talking, only more watching. Dad came back after the milking and told me, "The kids will be going to school. I'll take you home now to take care of the baby, then I'll stay here."

Mom stayed in the hospital until the soles of her feet peeled off and she was able to walk in fur slippers, then we brought her home. She didn't like the fact that we were always watching her. Her feelings of paranoia were justified. By this time, we all knew that something was seriously wrong.

One night, I heard some movement in our parents' bedroom. As I approached the doorway, I saw Mom's shadow on the wall. She was holding a butcher knife and had her arm raised, with the knife aimed at my father's sleeping body. I screamed, waking him up, and Mom backed into a corner. The knife was on the bed. We knew Mom was getting worse, and it felt that possibly we all were getting sick or crazy. Nothing changed, except Dad told us, "Be more careful. Stay out of the house, and get the barn work done." He continued to sleep in the same bed with Mom. I continued to take care of Tom and do the work in the house as usual.

SUMMER CAME, and we were busy with haymaking and picking strawberries, along with the usual milking and caring for the animals. One day, Dad came in and told me to get all the kids dressed up in their good clothes. (We each had two main outfits: good clothes for school and church, and barn overalls for working around the farm.) We loaded into our Model A Ford van, with Dad and Mom in the front, and went to the Lutheran church in Hancock. We all filed in, and we kids stayed in the dark, wooden entry room. I had a bottle of milk for Tom. We were quiet while Dad and Mom went in to meet with the minister.

We waited for what seemed like several hours. Finally, the door opened and Dad and Mom came out. Mom seemed crushed, and she was slumped over and crying. Then we all started to cry. That was a release, at least, that we could express our total sadness all together. There was a feeling among us of total hopelessness and helplessness. We couldn't keep on like this forever.

"What's going on?" someone asked. We were told, "Your mom is very sick. She's going through the change of life. This happens to women when they stop their periods." Well, I was skeptical. I didn't believe it had to be this way. Neither of my grandmothers had had this problem, my older teachers seemed to stay in school, my father's sisters were older—and they all seemed to age without problems like this.

After that church visit, Mom sat us on the front lawn and preached a sermon to us, telling us that we were all sinners and were going straight to hell. I heard this in church, along with other threatening statements. I was never much for the church after that.

We worked hard to find other kinds of help for Mom because the church alone wasn't doing it. The regular hospital wouldn't take her, and there were no beds in any mental hospital within 300 miles. I secretly wished we could make her comfortable in a jail cell, one where she couldn't hurt herself or us, and then we might all get some sleep.

Finally, the call came that there was a bed available at the Newberry Sanitarium, a mental hospital that was 200 miles away. I packed her bag. Uncle John, Aunt Asta, Dad, and I took her there to be admitted. There were no struggles or fights. We had a thermos of coffee with us and were able to make the trip in relative quiet. Maybe Mom also hoped for some help.

When we got to the sanitarium, Mother had to sign some admission papers. Absolutely not. She wouldn't sign. We waited for many hours, until it was late and near midnight before she finally signed. My God, it was terrible to see her being led down the hall. A nurse with a key ring the size of a basketball opened a series of heavy metal doors that then slammed shut with a jailhouse bang.

"Goodbye, Mom, I'm so sorry," I cried.

SOON SCHOOL started, and we began to settle into our new routines. It was great to be getting sleep again. I would fill a quart thermos with warm milk and some Karo syrup for Tom, who slept with me. When he cried, I would feed and change him. But otherwise, it was a restful time.

I was depressed and felt sure I'd never see my mother again. My aunts said, "It's alright, Margaret. She'll be back. It will be ok." I stayed home from school that year to keep the place going and to care for baby Tom.

Later in the fall we were allowed to visit Mother. Dad and I went. I packed a nice lunch of pasties (a Cornish meal of potatoes, beef, onions, turnips and carrots baked in a pie crust), and the weather was unusually warm. We stopped along a lakeshore and ate before we got to the hospital. I was so happy to be going to see her.

When we went through the doors of the sanitarium, I saw that Mother had her back to us, and she seemed to be looking out the window. I ran up and hugged her tightly. She was startled and stiffened when she looked at me.

"Hi, Mom."

She looked at me for a long moment and then said, "Who are you?"

"I'm Margaret, your daughter. Your baby is really growing and doing fine."

"What baby?"

"Tom. Tom is eight months old already. He's happy and crawling all over the place."

Silence.

Nothing.

Oh my God, what am I going to do now? I have to go home and tell the kids. What am I going to say?

I knew they did electroshock to treat depression, but what the hell happened? My dad talked to the nurse and the doctor. I don't know what they said, except Dad reported back that Mom would be there for several more months.

CHRISTMAS CAME and went. The kids still brought my homework to me each evening. I would do the assignments at night, and send the work to school with them in the morning.

I wanted to be a nurse, so I applied to attend the University of Michigan. When I was younger, at about age fourteen, I had represented our small school in Lansing during a state-wide student government meeting. I met a boy named Roger there. He was a wonderful student from lower Michigan, and was at the time the Michigan Boys State Governor. We liked each other and agreed that we would plan to meet again at the University of Michigan in Ann Arbor after high school.

Mom came home in the spring, and it was great to have her back. She was on medications that seemed to be helping her. She remembered who we were, but it wasn't like she was all well again. There were still a lot of issues.

We got back into the routine of walking on eggshells and being very careful not to create a stir. Mother took her medications. It seemed like we would eventually get used to the new routine. Then, one night, I heard something going on in our parents' bedroom downstairs. The bed was squeaking, squeaking, squeaking...

"Jesus Christ, they're having sex!" I started screaming like a crazy woman, just hollering. I heard Mom in her bathroom, then she came upstairs and asked me what was wrong. I said, "We can't have another baby here." She said, "You shouldn't worry, Marg. Things will be ok." I wasn't sure about that. I didn't know how to handle it.

Did I now think I needed to control my parents sex life?

Was I jealous?

Did I think I was the woman of the house?

Am I now the one who's crazy?

Did Mom feel she had to compete with me?

Mom started to resent the fact that we'd done well enough

at home without her. The baby was healthy, farm work got done, the kids were all in school, we were getting sleep, the cows were producing, the chickens were well again and laying plenty of eggs. Dad was more peaceful, controlled and determined to keep us all under one roof, though Aunt Asta still wanted us kids divided and farmed out to different relatives.

CHAPTER 2

LUCKY BREAKS

When Mom came home from the sanitarium, I went back to school. My biology teacher was quite interested when I told him about the chicken surgery I'd invented and performed. He said he'd never heard of someone doing that.

My math teacher, Mrs. Pearl, continued to encourage me to go to college. I told her that I'd written to the University of Michigan to request an application. When I got home, I asked my mother if it had arrived in the mail yet. She said my Dad had it, so I asked him for it. He brought it out and said, "Girls don't go to college. It's a waste of time to apply."

"Well," I said. "I just want to see the letter."

He slapped it on the table and said, "Don't expect a damned nickel from me."

I didn't say what was on my mind. I knew we didn't have a nickel to spare, but that was fine. I would find my own way.

The application was on green paper. I would fill it out if I could find the money to go.

I knew I had to find a better job, too, if I was going to save money for college. A few months later, when she was in a quieter place, my mother said, "You can go to California now, Marg. You're not needed here." Her sister—my aunt Helen—and her husband Bert owned a diner in Alameda, across the bay from San Francisco, and they needed some help. That's just what I wanted to hear. I had saved up $110 from my Broemer's job by then, and I bought a round-trip train ticket to San Francisco.

My aunt Ila and her husband lived in Alameda too. Helen and Ila were two of my mother's younger sisters. Helen was a nurse and became my mentor. I wanted to be just like her. She was present at my birth in Detroit. In fact, she had always told me what a beautiful sunny day that was, because I was born that day—May 6—and because she got her nursing diploma on that day.

Ila sent me very careful instructions about how to change trains in Chicago. I had never been away from home on my own, except for that trip to Lansing two years previously for the student government meeting.

The day of my departure came, and my sister Pat loaned me her red jumper, which I wore with a white blouse. It was evening, the end of May, and the sun was beginning to lower in the sky. The days were getting longer.

I had one leather suitcase full of salami and cheese sandwiches for the five-day trip, and another suitcase with all of my belongings. I said goodbye to Mom, picked up my suitcases, and started walking down Paradise Hill Road. I didn't want to cause a stir, so I didn't even say goodbye to the kids, who were out in the barn. That would be too hard.

I don't recall any emotions I had as I walked, though I know they were there. I knew if I let them out, I might not leave. The orange setting sun was behind me and there was a long shadow leading me on. I'd walked about a half a mile when I heard a car come up. It was my dad and the whole family, in the green Model A panel truck. "Need a lift?"

They took me the last mile to the train station. That was good. As I got on the train, my dad said, "Keep your nose clean." I still wonder what he meant by that. Don't cry? Don't mind other peoples' business? What?

Steam poured out of the train stack, the whistle blew, and we rounded the bend out of Chassell. I had $10 to my name.

IN CHICAGO, I had a six-hour layover at a larger station. I didn't want to fall asleep and miss my train, so I went into the women's restroom to kill time. There was a woman there, bending over to clean the toilets. I waited until she straightened up and then asked her if she needed any help.

She looked surprised, and asked me what was wrong with me. I told her I had six hours to wait until my train left and I could help. "Honey," she said, "I've worked here for 30 years and no one ever offered to help. You need to rest. I have a room on the 24th floor right here in this train station. I will take you there and will wake you up in time to catch your train." It was a small room with a single bed and a window covered with a dark shade. I didn't sleep, but it felt good to stretch out.

The woman came to get me with plenty of time to board my train. As it slowly pulled out of Chicago, I was seated next to the window. I had never imagined there could be so many trains in one place. I was amazed that I had gotten on the right train and was heading in the right direction.

I didn't eat for a few meals. I was embarrassed to open my case of sandwiches, so I waited until everyone was in the dining car and then took my suitcase into the restroom. The restrooms on the trains were bigger then. There was a little sitting area for lounging. I ate there, and got a drink of water from the tap. After a few days on the train, some people told me they were worried that I wasn't eating, and asked me to join them in the dining car. I didn't want to get stuck with the bill, so I told them I was doing ok and not to worry.

Finally, we reached the San Francisco station. The air was moist and I smelled the salt from the ocean, which was a very different smell from the pure air of Lake Superior. Pigeons welcomed me with cooing and droppings. Aunt

Helen arrived in a red Pontiac. That evening, I took Pat's red jumper off. I was shocked to find that my white blouse and all my underwear had turned red from sweating for five days on the train.

I LOVED CALIFORNIA and I loved my aunts. After a few months, they suggested that I might like to finish my last year of high school in Alameda. I called Mom and asked her permission. Her voice was soft as she said, "Yes, that's ok, Marg." My mom had been the smartest kid in her class growing up in Pilgrim, a few miles from our farm. She, too, had gone to work when she was thirteen. She, too, had to stay home from school to care for her mother. She took care of seven siblings after her mother had a ruptured appendix. After several months, my mother went back to doing housework in Hancock. Although she loved school, she wasn't able to attend after the eighth grade. She taught us kids to read before we went to kindergarten and always stressed the importance of furthering our education.

One evening in Alameda, I was walking home after school when I noticed a sign out in front of the Alameda General Hospital. It had a picture of the president of the hospital, Mr. Brookhouser. I walked in and asked to see the President. The receptionist took me to his office. I told Mr. Brookhouser my story—that I was in California to earn money for college, that I wanted to be a nurse, that my family was in Michigan, and that I needed a job. He smiled, paused, and looked at me over his glasses. "Let me call Mrs. Driscoll," he said.

Within three minutes, Mrs. Driscoll was in the office. "This young lady," he began, and he gave Mrs. Driscoll my spiel. "Do you have a job for her?" Mrs. Driscoll wore a white lab coat and had blond hair and a nice smile. "Sure," she said. "She can start on Saturday."

I started at the hospital with a job in the laboratory filing pathology specimens. They were interesting—appendix, brain, liver, heart—a human heart! My heart was pounding as I started doing the work, because it was great.

Next, I learned to do urinalyses, draw blood, and do EKGs up on the floor! Now I was at the patients' bedsides, and working with real people. I learned so much.

I would eat lunch with the nurses in the hospital cafeteria. Miss Poffenberger was the chief nurse. She asked me how I'd gotten the job. When I told her I wanted to be a nurse, she heaved back in her chair and said, "Don't be a nurse. You want to be a doctor! Then you can make all of your own decisions and be the boss." The seed was planted. I had never thought of being a doctor before. Her reaction to what I wanted to do was certainly different from my father's dismissive, "Girls don't go to college."

In California, I met all sorts of people who wanted to adopt or marry me. My high school English teacher wanted me to live with her in Berkeley, and even said she would pay my way to the University of California. My math teachers and others tutored me, and showed me how I was growing and improving. They all wanted me to succeed.

Then there was a young man named Art Leydecker, who was a regular in my aunt's diner. We started dating. He had an airplane and took me for flights over California's San Joaquin Valley and the mountains. We went to restaurants and football games in San Francisco. His mother wanted him to find a nice girl and get married. On the day I met her, she and Art pulled out a huge diamond ring. I had never seen anything like it. It seemed the size of a marble, and the sparkle had a slight bluish cast. Art asked me if I wanted it. Was he proposing marriage or what? I almost fainted. Of course I couldn't imagine wearing a thing like that. No one wore any rings on the farm. It would be dangerous, a hazard when working around farm machinery. I can't remember how I got out of it—most likely by being in a big hurry. That was the end of our airplane flights. Remembering Art now, I wonder about him. I felt so safe with him and yet I don't ever recall kissing him. I hope he found a nice girl or guy, and happiness and love.

JUNE—AND HIGH SCHOOL graduation—was coming up fast. Although I'd been accepted at the University of

Michigan, my friend Roger from our student government days backed out of our date to meet in Ann Arbor. He'd decided to attend DePauw University in Indiana because "Michigan is too large," he said.

I got a call around then from Wilmer Savela, our high school principal in my hometown in Michigan. He asked when I would be coming home. I told him June 15. "Will you run for strawberry queen? The Lions want to sponsor you." I didn't have anything big planned for the summer, and I still had time to make a white dress and paint some strawberries on the skirt, so I said, "Yes, I'll run." I would need three outfits: one to speak with the Judges, another for meet and greet, and a formal gown for the final and the parade.

I had a formal gown that Sarah, a family friend, had made. Sarah was on our egg delivery route and later became my stepmother. I borrowed another dress from my sister Pat. There were seven contestants and I won! The governor of Michigan at the time, G. Mennen "Soapy" Williams (heir to the Mennen shaving cream fortune), was on hand for the crowning. Afterward I had to go to Escanaba to the Upper Peninsula Fair, and I won there, too. My dad was beginning to wonder what was going on? How could his daughter be winning these contests?

After the fair in Escanaba, I was expected to go on next to Detroit for the State Fair contest. The demands on my time as the Fair Queen were beginning to be a problem. I was expected to be at university in a week, and I had exhausted my sister Pat's wardrobe. I didn't have any fresh clothes to wear. People from the Lions Club and the local business community told me to go to Gartner's, a department store in Hancock, and pick out three dresses and they would pay for them. I got dresses that would also work for college.

There were 22 women candidates at the State Fair contest. Some of them were of a different caliber than those of us who were farm girls. They were older, more experienced, and more made up. Also, the judges took their jobs more seriously at the State Fair. When they announced the winner, I almost fainted when it was *my* name they called. I phoned to tell my mother and she asked, "Well what did you do for the talent part?" She knew I didn't sing, didn't dance except for the polka (I would wear through the soles of three pairs of shoes every summer), and had no talent on the piano. "Nothing," I said. "I just talked, told them about the farm and about my trip to California and that I was planning to be a doctor." Dad was angry again. "Now I suppose she'll end up in burlesque!" I did win a scholarship to the Powers Modeling School, but that wasn't going to help me where I was headed: medical school.

AT THE UNIVERSITY of Michigan, all freshmen had to live in the dormitory for the first year. I had saved a little over $1000 and that got me through room, board, books, and tuition for the first semester.

I enjoyed my courses. Zoology was terrific. By my second semester, I was a teaching assistant in the zoology lab. I did well in my courses—except for English composition. The teacher's assistant kept giving us assignments to write papers, about anything. This really caused me to panic. I was paralyzed. I didn't have a word to say.

"Well, what was your family like?" the TA asked.

I told him a bunch of lies and stories like how great life was on the farm. He said, "That's wonderful, write about that."

"What movies do you like to see?" he asked.

"None," I told him. "They're a waste of time."

"What did you read as a child?"

"Nothing."

The more questions he asked, the more the anxiety and paralysis set in, and I started to get depressed about English Comp. I spent a lot of time in the library looking up subjects I could write about. Nothing seemed to relate to my life. I scraped through with a D+. That trauma hasn't made a huge difference in my life, but up to that point I had never struggled that much in anything. I started to feel guilty about leaving home and wondered how the kids were doing and how Mom was doing. I was out of money anyway, so maybe... oh well.

After the first semester, I went to see the Dean of Women, Deborah Bacon, and told her my whole story. Afterwards, she walked out of her office and was gone for a couple of minutes. When she came back, she sat closer to me, on a chair on my side of the desk. "Margaret, I have made arrangements for you to have full tuition paid for as long as you want to study here at Michigan. You don't need to stay in the dormitory. There is a bed available in a women's co-op house on Forest Avenue." I was shocked. "Good luck to you," she said. A few days later, I got a letter from her confirming our conversation. I still have that letter.

DURING SCHOOL BREAKS, I would hitch a ride home to the farm with Paul Kangas, who lived in Houghton near Chassell. But home was not the same. Baby Tom was no longer a baby. Everyone had jobs, and hardly anyone was around. All I remember is squatting in a dark corner on that visit, feeling sad and not talking. My mother said, "Why don't you go and talk to the neighbors. Mrs. Haapala would love to see you." I felt lonely, yet I didn't do anything about it.

During that first year at university, Mom had a number of readmissions to Newberry Sanitarium, and they seemed to go easier than the first time. Dad continued having intense and sometimes volatile reactions to minor things, like when kids would gather together and start laughing or goofing off. I was always glad to go back to school after spending my breaks at home.

School kept me busy. I took comparative anatomy as a freshman, and by the time I was a sophomore I was teaching pre-med students. I was also pre-med, so this gave me a chance to know who would be in my class in medical school. By December of my third year, I applied for early admission to the University of Michigan's medical school.

I was taking a bluebook final in economics that year when I saw that a fellow pre-med student was also taking the test. I had noticed him around campus several times. He was tall, fair-haired, and looked sort of like a Finn from my hometown. He seemed confident in his stride, and he was usually with a girl. I'd often seen him in the library. He wore glasses, but with one lens missing. I knew that because he would sometimes rub his eye with a finger right through the frame. I didn't have a lot to say about economic theory during that test, but the guy I was watching kept writing like a madman until the bell rang. When he got up, I ran after him and started a conversation as we climbed the stairs out of Angell Hall.

At the top of the stairs, we ran into John McFatridge, who was a fellow student in my comparative anatomy class. John had always wanted to set me up with a certain frat brother he said he knew I'd love. "He's tall and smart and...." Blah, blah, blah. I'd heard it all before. When John saw us, he started hollering, "This is Ross! This is the guy I wanted you to meet! I didn't know you knew each other."

I was singing with the Michigan Chorale in the Magnificat that night, so Ross and I set up our first date. He came to the concert and afterward we went to Drake's for limeades and grilled cinnamon buns. Going to Drake's was fabulous, because it meant I didn't have to worry about him getting drunk and wanting to have sex.

Ross and I started dating that week before the Christmas holidays. We decided to keep our Christmases with the folks short and return to Ann Arbor early while the other students were still gone. Then we could spend more time together before school started again. We thought about each other all the time. It was great that the thirty pounds I'd gained during my first two years on campus didn't seem to bother Ross. I'd been eating ice cream to cover up my worries about home, Mom, and English composition.

That Christmas break at home was terrific. I told Mom that I'd met a guy I really loved. "How long have you been dating?" she asked.

"Well, I only met him last week, and I'm going back early to see him again," I told her.

Back in Ann Arbor after being home for Christmas, Ross had Wildcat, one of his fraternity buddies, make a steak dinner for us at the Phi Gam house. Not only did he make a delicious meal, Wildcat also serenaded us with his ukulele. No one else was around and it was just amazing. Ross had come back to campus with the family car, a navy blue Chrysler. His father had been an English professor at the University of Alaska and now he wrote speeches for the president of the Chrysler Corporation. Did I say English professor? *Oh, my!*

A day later, while still on Christmas break, Ross took me to Birmingham, Michigan, to meet his parents and his two younger sisters. I loved his mother, Margaret. She told me that I knew her kitchen better than she did when I whipped up breakfast and muffins for the family breakfast. She was a science editor at the nearby Cranbrook Institute. Ross had two sisters. Martha was an undergraduate student at the University of Michigan as well, and Susan was still in high school. They laughed a lot, said anything they wanted to say, and their clothes weren't homemade. We all went together to see *Oklahoma*, but I don't remember if it was the movie or live.

IN ANN ARBOR, I was living on Washtenaw Avenue, in the home of Wilbur and Maxine Pierpont. Mr. Pierpont was the vice president for finance at the University of Michigan. His name was on all the checks paid to university employees, and he was responsible for much of the growth and expansion of the University during that time. I had a free room and breakfast with the family, in exchange for ironing seven to ten shirts a week and occasional babysitting. The Pierponts were family and home to me.

From the Pierponts' house, I walked past the Phi Gam house each morning. Ross was always waiting for me, in rain or snow. I never had to carry my books to school again.

Ross and I were both accepted to medical school to start the next fall. Before then, Ross had wanted to meet my family. I told him about Mom, and warned him about my dad, saying that he was volatile and that we hadn't spoken much since I'd left home four years ago. Ross wanted to meet them anyway, so when we had some days off in February, he borrowed his folks' car and we drove like crazy to the straits of Mackinaw. There was no bridge then, and the moment we got to the Straits, the last ferry had just pulled away from the dock. We'd missed it.

Ross got a huge smile on his face. "Guess we have to get a room in a motel in Mackinaw City," he said. Well now, this would be interesting. I wasn't about to lose my virginity on a cold night in Michigan before I was married. My Finnish parents raised me with the fear of God and stern, Victorian rules. Anyway, we rolled around a lot and finally got some sleep before we caught the first ferry in the morning. Years later, when I was talking to our adolescent sons about sex, I told them that I hadn't had sex before I was married. They asked me more questions and I described some dates like that one Ross and I had in Mackinaw City. Our son David said, "Mom, that's sex. Don't kid yourself."

After a couple of slides into ditches and snow banks, we arrived at my family's home in time for the evening milking. Ross went into the barn with my dad. Dad wasn't one to do much talking, so I wondered what was Ross going to do. "He could shovel manure," I thought to myself. "That's a quick learn." Ross came into the house about two hours later, took me aside, and said, "Your dad is the greatest." I waited for the next word of his sentence and then asked, "Greatest what?" Ross said, "You have no idea how much he loves you. He told me you were the perfect kid to raise. He said, 'I never had a moment's worry about her' and waxed on and on."

Now this was interesting. Did Ross think I was a liar? Or was Ross a liar?

Ross loved my mother. And she loved him! She really went all out to cook the finest food our farm had to offer. It was just our ordinary food like we had on Sundays—venison, or roast chicken, mashed potatoes, mashed turnips, homemade bread and apple pie—but, for Ross, it was the greatest of gourmet meals. I don't know what he was comparing it to.

BACK IN ANN ARBOR in February, Ross and I were eating banana splits at the Kresge dime store counter and I mentioned that my friend Annie had been wondering when we were getting married. Ross said he was wondering, too. We had a short discussion and quickly decided it would be better to marry before we started medical school in September. It would be cheaper to buy one set of books and to share groceries, which we could buy on Saturdays when the perishables went on sale at the A&P on State

Street. We'd find a cheap apartment to share. I would cook and Ross would wash dishes, we decided, though it didn't work out that way in the end. He found out that I could cook a meal in quick order, but that it took forever to do the dishes. He did the laundry on weekends, instead. Anyway, I was sold. That first winter of living together, we ran track in one of the University's indoor gymnasiums. In my newfound love and happiness I lost 35 pounds of ice cream fat.

This was during my third year as an undergrad. I still had to take organic chemistry in the summer before starting medical school. Ross worked at Equipment Manufacturing Inc., loading racks on front-end loaders for heavy equipment all that summer. He commuted to Detroit from Birmingham by bicycle to earn enough money for a wedding ring, and to save up some dough for school. We skipped our senior year of college, and therefore did not actually get our Bachelors of Science degrees, but went straight on to medical school.

We budgeted $100 for wedding expenses, and that included the material for the dresses and a three-layer cake. On weekends, I would sort through remnants in Hudson's department store in Detroit, looking for lace and material for my wedding dress and the bridesmaids' dresses.

We were married in the small Lutheran church next to my high school in Chassell. People in the community brought ham, salads, pastries, and other homemade dishes. Ross' dad told us we had to have Jim Beam whiskey, so he bought it. Somehow, we managed to pay for a terrific hometown polka band. Everyone came. The minister must have spoken in Finnish (my parents' native tongue), because I don't remember a word he said. And how would Ross know what the minister said? He was just waiting to kiss me after it was over. After the ceremony, we all walked to the community center, where we had the reception, did some wild dancing, and joked around.

Baby Tom was six when I got married, and everyone else was growing up, too. I sent $35 to my brother Willie shortly afterward, so he could get a bus ticket to leave the farm. He worked in Detroit for a year, and then he joined the Army.

After the wedding, I went downstairs, took off my gown, and packed it carefully in a garbage bag. I haven't seen it since. Must have gone out with the rest of the trash. Maybe that was good luck for us, because the marriage itself has always been looked after and cared for by both of us since that day.

CHAPTER 3

MEDICAL SCHOOL / THE HONEYMOON'S OVER

Medical school started on September 12, 1957. Ross and I had thought it was September 13. On the first day of medical school, we were still on our honeymoon, driving home from visiting Mount Rainier and the national parks out west, when the dean had taken roll call. This was serious because anyone who was discovered absent could lose their place that day to a hopeful student from the wait list. Alphabetically, Ross Fletcher was called first. No answer. Then Margaret Mackrain. No answer. One of my friends from comparative anatomy who was also in the lecture hall yelled out, "She married the other person who isn't here, and I know they're going to be here. I guess I also know what they're doing right now."

When we arrived a day late, we still had our spots. There was a stir in the office when I told them my last name had changed to Fletcher, because the class groupings had already been arranged in alphabetical order. They wanted us to be kept apart during the program, because a previous couple had fought during their anatomy dissection lab. We didn't have a car, so we rode our bikes about four miles to class. It would be a problem if we had different schedules and days off, especially for handling chores together like grocery shopping. The Dean's office approved us to be in the same group and have the same class schedule.

There were twelve women and 200 men in our class. Eight of the women would graduate, along with about 180 men.

We consistently had great professors, which was quite different from some of the undergraduate classes I'd taken. Anatomy was my favorite class, along with biochemistry. In anatomy, six students were assigned to each cadaver. We came to love our cadaver, this guy who'd given his body for us to learn from. I'd enjoyed learning about the evolution of changes from the shark to the cat in comparative anatomy—and now to the human.

Ross and I studied a lot, all the time. He would really get alarmed when he heard me reciting the origins and insertions of muscles in my sleep. "My God, she's studying in her sleep." We had a large poster of the Krebs cycle over our kitchen table. We ate, napped, and studied until eleven or twelve every night, and went to school all day. On Saturdays, Ross would ride us on his bicycle, with me sitting on the crossbar, to a football game, or to a movie if the Wolverines were playing a game out of town. We would go to the Dairy Queen and eat ice cream sandwiches for a Sunday treat between study sessions when we had to get out for air.

MEDICAL SCHOOL was fun. It was difficult, but life was simple: work, study, sleep, eat, and not much else, except passing the tests and other exams.

I worked in the surgical research lab to earn money for food and books. Our project was to study the various medications and ion exchange resins in hypertensive liver failure on dogs with portacaval shunts. I did the surgical procedures in our lab. It was quite complicated vascular work to connect the portal vein to the inferior vena cava. I got a reputation because I could do the procedure in 17 minutes from the time I opened the skin until the last stitch was put in to close the skin, surpassing fellows with many more years of surgery experience. That was fun, and, even then, I thought my skill might have been a gift.

In September of our last year of medical school, I told Ross that we didn't have to worry any more. "Worry about what?" he asked.

"About getting pregnant before we're done with school," I said. "It's nine months now until we graduate."

"Great!" said Ross.

Our son John was born two days after Edward R. Murrow gave our graduation address in the Michigan Stadium. My cap and gown was a nice maternity outfit. Climbing the stadium stairs was not so nice.

John being born seemed like a miracle. After studying all that can go wrong in fetal development in our embryology class, we'd saved up $1500 in case our baby needed heart surgery, cleft palate repair or anything else, because we didn't have any health insurance. But John was perfect. We spent the money on a down payment for our first house instead, which cost $12,000. Ross' parents gave us an old Plymouth, which we nicknamed the Green Latrine. We moved down Miller Road to Creal Crescent, a community of other young doctors in training, one that had a lot of babies and wonderful home childcare nearby.

We were each on call in the hospital every other night, so Ross would be with John while I was overnight in the hospital, and I would be with John the next night. Dishes got washed on Saturdays. I cooked on Sundays whenever I wasn't in the hospital. We found a way to make it work.

I wanted to know how I was going to raise a family over the next 20 years and do surgery at the same time, so I went to ask Dr. Norman Miller, the chairman of Obstetrics and Gynecology. He said, "No way. You give up the family or you do something else besides being a obstetric surgeon."

My next stop was in orthopedics. Professor Badgley remembered a woman who had been in his department during World War II when the men were overseas. That had worked out, so he told me I could join him any time.

Dr. Work, Chairman of Otolaryngology, told me, "Margaret, there are about five good women otolaryngologists in the country. I can make you one of the best, and you can have a family, too."

That sounded good to me. I'd loved the intricate anatomy in the head and neck, and I loved the fun I had on my rotations in otolaryngology (also called ENT, for *ear*, *nose*, and *throat*). It was possible to make amazing diagnoses about conditions that were well-hidden from the eyes of other doctors.

When I was a student and working at the hospital, a patient came in and wanted to see the eye doctor because his left eye kept tearing. I told him the eye clinic was down the hall, but I would be glad to see him anyway. I noticed a very small red mass the size of a small pea coming out above one of the bones in his nose. I biopsied it there in the clinic and ordered x-rays, which showed some clouding in the sinus. I sent him to ophthalmology for an eye exam and then moved on to another rotation. While in the new rotation, I was called back to ENT. I wondered if I had done something wrong. Instead, the chief resident told me I had made an amazing diagnosis of cancer of the maxillary sinus, and if the person had been sent out without a thorough examination like I had given, it might have delayed the diagnosis for several months.

As we finished medical school, we went through the process of matching our medical school education with a hospital interested in having us for internship and possibly residency training. This is like football draft, with teams picking and choosing the football players they want. Ross and I visited several hospitals together, such as Bellevue, Cornell, and New York Presbyterian in New York. In the end, we decided we wanted to stay in Ann Arbor.

The results came in on internship matching day, and Ross and I were both matched for internship training at the University of Michigan in Ann Arbor. However, Dr. Towsley, Professor of Pediatrics, matched me with pediatrics instead of surgery. Surgery was still considered macho—and for men. Professors felt women were well-suited for psychiatry or pediatrics—caring for children—which I agree is wonderful. But I wanted to do surgery, so I rejected my internship match at the University of Michigan Hospital. Dr. Brown, the Surgery Chief at St. Joseph's Hospital, two blocks away from the university hospital, agreed to accept my application. I did my two years of general surgery training in the surgery department there. Many University of Michigan surgery professors were also on staff at St. Joseph's, including the medical school's dean, Dr. A. Furstenberg, and Professor Reed Dingman, the chairman of Plastic Surgery. I had an excellent two years of surgery training. On July 1st, 1963, I went back to the University of Michigan for my specialty: otolaryngology surgical training.

Our second son, Jim, was born during my ENT residency. When Dr. Work heard about my pregnancy, he called me into his office. "I do not want to hear about these things through the grapevine," he said. "If you get pregnant, I want to be the first to know."

Around that time, residents had a 30-day vacation allowance. My month off started the day Jim was born, so staffing didn't have to change much. Being pregnant didn't bother me while doing surgery–I was in good physical shape–but the stench of doing nasal surgery made me nauseated in my first trimester.

IN FEBRUARY of 1966, Ross got a letter that would change our lives. He was told to report to the Sam Houston Army Training Center in one month for basic training. He would be 30 that July, so the U.S. Army grabbed him to serve in the Vietnam War while he was still within the age limits. In just five more months, he would have aged out of the draft. He had not yet finished his residency. I was pregnant with our third child, David, and would also finish my residency on June 30.

Damn, things had been going so smoothly. What the hell?

No amount of talking or pleading with the authorities worked to change the situation, but it wasn't as bad as it had seemed. After Ross went through basic training, he was stationed at the Pentagon, which was much better than going to Vietnam, of course. If he turned out to be a good doctor, useful to the generals with their heart problems, he might even be able to stay in Washington, D.C. for the whole two years of his service.

Ross left Ann Arbor to go to boot camp in March. Our third son, David, was born on May 1st, and I got the whole month of May off. I'd already sold the house, and on May 3rd the boys and I flew into National Airport in Washington, D.C. Ross met me and had two cars waiting–one for him and the three boys and one for me. We were going to drive to Chesapeake Beach, where he had rented a house for a month. We needed two cars so he could get back to work each day in D.C., and so I would have a car if I had an emergency. As we drove our little caravan through the D.C. traffic, I began to feel sick. I hadn't had a rest or food all day, and I was probably dehydrated as well. I drove on anyway.

On the drive to the Chesapeake, I saw nothing but trees—beautiful, yes. I saw some dogwoods starting to bloom, but no stores, no people, nothing. At one point, I stopped the car in a ditch and laid on the horn until Ross got out of the other car and came over. "Where in the hell are we going?" I asked him. "I can't do this." "Oh honey," he said. "We're almost there. You're going to love it. Believe me, we'll go to a restaurant and get some crabs. You'll love them." That drive was so hard it reminded me of our mountain-climbing excursions that often lasted beyond the point of total exhaustion.

We did get there, finally, and Ross carried me from the car into the house, where he laid me on the bed with some Rice Krispy treats he produced from under the seat of the car, which our neighbor in Ann Arbor had given him three months ago when he left home. He was right. I loved it at Chesapeake Beach. Each day, I loaded the buggy with baby and food and boys, and spent the day looking for shark teeth and turtles on the beach with the kids while Ross went to work in the Pentagon.

That month of vacation went fast. During that time, we often took excursions around D.C. on weekends to find a house we could live in when I finished residency at the end of June. We found a small, split-level house in Calverton, Maryland. I also looked for a job at Georgetown University Hospital, in Washington, D.C. The Chief of Otalaryngology there said he had never worked with a woman surgeon, and that no positions were open. I knew of two University of Michigan people who were now at the University of Maryland Hospital: Dr Blanchard, Professor of Otolaryngology, and Dr. Buxton, the Chief of Surgery. I went there to interview with them–and I got a job.

Then the boys and I went back to Ann Arbor for a month to finish my residency.

I AM LEARNING a lot as I sit here and write to you, Shana.

Why did I go back back to Ann Arbor?

Why didn't I just take another month off? I could have.

I really needed time to move to Maryland and time to rest. What I did not need was to struggle alone with three kids and my surgical residency for another month. You have taught me this, Shana. These are issues about women's and family rights.

When I left Ann Arbor on June 30, after finishing my residency, we had not yet moved into the new house in Maryland. We had no babysitter, no food, nothing in place. I asked Dr. Blanchard if I could start work in mid-July.

"All residents and doctors start on July first." Dr. Blanchard said. "I need you on July first. Plus, I haven't had a vacation in six years, so I'm out of here. As soon as you get here, you can run this department while I'm gone. You can call me if you have a problem."

So there I was, on July 1, 1966, teaching twelve new doctors how to be head and neck surgeons, starting just one day after finishing my own residency.

CHAPTER 4

LIKE MOTHER, LIKE DAUGHTER

There I was, Shana, having been a wife for nine years, a doctor for five years. I was the mother of three sons, an otorhinolaryngologist, and a head and neck surgeon. I had twelve years of college behind me. I was in Washington, D.C. How the hell did I get here? It wasn't what I'd expected.

Washington D.C. was so different from Ann Arbor. The cars were going in all directions and the signs on the roads seemed to show up only when it was too late to see them. The only way I knew how to get around was to start at National Airport, and then aim for where I was headed. If I got lost, I would go back to the airport and start over. I thought I should be happy, but I felt lost all the time, and had those sad feelings I'd had when I started college. Studies, marriage, kids, degrees—all those things had kept me going. There was much happiness, and there was so much to be grateful for. So why the sadness?

When I remember being twelve and seeing my mom curled up with sadness on the davenport, and with more sadness after Tom was born, it makes me wonder if I also had post-partum depression during the time after I arrived in D.C.

WHEN ROSS' parents and I first met, I had drinks with them. That's when I had started drinking. We couldn't afford alcohol when we were students, so I drank more than my share when we went to parties and the drinks were free. After those parties, I often ended up vomiting in the host's bushes. I thought I was allergic to the shrimp. When we moved to the D.C. area, we lived in the suburbs. The neighbors would come over for daiquiris on the weekends, and sometimes in the evenings, if I got home early enough.

Ross was still in the Army. He would come home from work around 5:30, for the boys. John was five when we moved to D.C., Jim was three, and David was two months old. A neighbor kid took care of them during the day until I found a woman we called Aunt Kay, who lived in our neighborhood with some relatives. She was a very kind and patient soul. She had twin girls who were six, so with all our kids combined we had a houseful, and a big back yard for them to play in.

Although I was now teaching Head and Neck Surgery in the Otolaryngology Department at the University of Maryland Hospital, I needed to take the board exams of the American Academy of Otolaryngology in order to be a certified Fellow of the Academy, and a properly trained specialist. The exams were held in Chicago, at the Palmer House, in September of 1967. The lifelong certification is a required credential to practice anywhere as a specialist. There were three days of oral exams and two days of written exams. I went to Chicago with about 200 pounds of books, a microscope, pathology slides, notes, and x-rays. I was ready for anything they wanted to throw at me.

During my boards, a professor asked me what I would do if presented with a patient who had swallowed lye. He tossed up the x-rays on the light box and I told him what I would do. He then tossed up the x-rays of the esophagus after the treatment and asked me what had gone wrong. I told him that the second x-rays belonged to someone else–the names on them were different. He was shocked, looked at the x-rays, then said, "Shit, get out of here!" So that was the end of that session.

I went into the next room to meet a different examiner and waited a good while, which worried me. These sessions were all timed, and my time was being chewed up by waiting. I walked out into the hall and saw five professors in a huddle. I heard them discussing who would come and examine me. Doctor Baker from Columbia Presbyterian said, "I'll go. I don't mind giving her an A if she deserves it." He came and presented some more information about patients for me to discuss how I would care for them. Then I took the written examinations for a couple of days, and I was done.

When I got home, I got a call from Dr. Work, my mentor at Michigan, saying that I'd gotten the second highest score in the country on the board exams. I missed being first by four tenths of a point.

IN 1968, Ross finished his term with the Army. He wanted all of us to go on a trip to Europe. He'd been there while in the Army, on some congressional boondoggle, as the group's physician. He loved all the new countries. So off we went. David was almost two at the time. We landed in London, where we visited our friend Tom Preston. Tom loaned us his Volkswagen beetle and in it we left for France. We were in Europe for a month and visited nine countries. It was great traveling with Ross and the boys. John was old enough and good enough with math to be able to take care of all the currency exchanges and food purchases. People running the pensions where we stayed often offered to look after the boys when Ross and I went out for dinner.

When we were in the Alps, I noticed that I couldn't button my clothes or reach my arms around to my back. I also couldn't find shoes that were comfortable. Then I started to get a fever and it felt like my body wanted to shut down. I had pain in my hands, wrists, ankles, and feet. My legs felt like they were full of cement. I drank more double cappuccinos in the morning to get going, and I drank double martinis at night to get to sleep. I also started to note that my hands and feet were often swollen. I was shocked and said to Ross, "Do you think this could be rheumatoid arthritis?" He said he didn't know, but it could be. We rarely agreed on diagnoses we made on our kids, but the signs were there for agreement on this one. I figured that was probably from not getting enough rest. I pushed it all aside and kept going.

When we landed back in D.C., we saw the newspapers and learned that Martin Luther King Jr. had been shot. The city seemed to be on fire, and people were just trying to survive. I hated to leave the boys at home to go to work. Baltimore was also on fire. Men were hitting each other with metal pipes, and no one seemed to care who was killed. My boss, Dr. Blanchard, said that he wasn't going to worry until they started coming after him. It seemed as though the world—including my body—was coming apart all at once.

Eventually, things settled down enough that our lives went on.

SURGERY AND teaching at the University of Maryland Hospital went well. I loved being in the operating room where it was quiet, and things ran smoothly. But there was one problem: There was too much lag time between surgical procedures. Nurses and anesthesia staff (and probably doctors too) would take long coffee breaks between cases and a lot of procedures had to be cancelled each day. The patients would have to stay in the hospital then, and hope they could be added to an already full schedule the following day.

The staff wouldn't change their lax habits because their salaries were the same whether they worked efficiently or not. Instead of waiting for other staff members to get busy and do their jobs, I started doing more of the work. I would take the patients from the operating room to the recovery rooms myself, remove dirty linens from the operating table, scrub the table and floor, and even make the bed. I'd get another patient into the operating room and get set up to go forward with the next surgery within ten minutes of the last patient leaving. Pretty soon, following my example, the operating room staff started showing up in a hurry, and the lag time between procedures shortened. My reputation spread, and Dr. Bordley from Johns Hopkins Hospital in Baltimore called and asked me to join the faculty there.

I took the job. My commute and time I spent away from the kids was longer, but I enjoyed more happiness at Hopkins, and the opportunities were greater. I did miss the ruggedness of the University of Maryland hospital, where the clinics were old, with worn hardwood floors, and there was an original Otis elevator that had no doors, only an open cage.

Meanwhile, the parties and my drinking got to be a bigger issue. My drinks changed from daiquiries in stemmed glasses to straight alcohol in coffee mugs, maybe even to sneaking drinks hidden in paper cups. It was not possible to drink and do otolaryngology and surgery at the same time, because when I was examining a patient, our heads would be close together—they could smell me and I could smell them. I also found it treacherous to do intricate surgery the morning after drinking a lot the night before. Doing ear surgery with a 40-power microscope—and with the shakes multiplied 40 times, too, because of the alcohol I'd drunk—was not possible. So I didn't schedule surgeries on Mondays anymore.

One Saturday, I was setting up for a party at home and got a phone call. Ross picked up. It was my dad. Ross looked ashen and handed me the phone. I heard my dad's voice as he said, "Mom died today, Margaret. She was feeling well, so I went to town to deliver the eggs. She even walked up Paradise Road yesterday."

"What happened?" I asked.

"She died by fire. She left a note. It just said, 'I'm sorry it had to end like this. Love, Ann.'"

I couldn't believe it. I couldn't believe the note either. *Oh my God. Oh my God.* It really did happen. Mom had been battling this problem for over 20 years. Just three weeks ago she had been in Maryland with us. At the time she seemed happy. She'd come down to be with me at Johns Hopkins, where she was hospitalized for a while. X-rays had shown that she had long-standing, advanced rheumatoid arthritis. There was extensive bone and cartilage loss in all of her joints. It always took her a long time to get up to answer the phone whenever I called, so Dad or Tom always answered first.

I wondered if she'd had rheumatoid arthritis all her life. Was that why she was depressed?

Mom's lab assays for rheumatoid arthritis were off the charts, but she'd never once complained of joint pain. She didn't complain of pain in her swollen hands, either. She hadn't wanted to stay with us very long after her hospitalization at Hopkins. While she was in Maryland, she would call Dad and tell him how much she missed him and Tom, and say that she wanted to go home.

Now she was gone.

I left the party to Ross and took the next flight out of Baltimore to northern Michigan. I'm sorry to say that I also packed a gallon of rum in my large suitcase. What was I thinking?

At home, no one wanted rum. No one wanted to eat. We were all sick. I didn't sleep and my shoulders would seize up. Probably from carrying my heavy suitcase. I ran around cleaning things up (another way of covering up the pain). Twenty years passed before I could even talk or really think about all of this.

ASHES

March came in with dancing shoes
He made the hilltops bare,
the lakes and rivers full.
He made mud for the tractors in the fields.
He cleaned the dead branches
from the trees.
The buds were red and ready.
He made maple syrup for breakfast.
He wakens the smelt in the full streams.
He pushes the ice out to sea.
He made a spot for trees and lady's slippers.
The silent stirring in her soul.
The winters dead and winters leaving.
March came in with dancing shoes.
She will do some cleaning.
She gathered useless trash.
She gathered precious memories.
She heaped them in a pile.
A volcano burst—
and lit the pile
where she was standing.
The fire and ashes flew

and settled on her body.
Were there memories, like the
warm spring day when I was born hungry,
when the radio was playing somewhere over the rainbow?
Did she remember the camping trip
when she first heard about him from his sisters?
Did she remember bath time with him
When I would play with buttons and listen
To Fibber Magee and Molly while
They had a nice bath?
Did she call for help?
Could she move?
The chickadees were chickadee-dee deeing in the trees.
I am left in her house
with ashes ever settling,
with blame and guilt as
my friends for coffee every day.
Or was it March in dancing shoes
with promise of the prom—
there was no dancing left in her.
There was somewhere over the rainbow
when the volcano blew.
In the ashes and the embers
I have found the soul she left me.

AFTER THE funeral was over, I started fixing things in the house where I'd grown up, to make it nice for my dad. The window was open and my sisters were out back. I heard one of them say my name and then the other one said, "I think she's crazy."

I got it. I got it. Yes, they were right. I did feel crazy, like a clown trying to keep twenty spinning plates on rods from falling. I did feel depressed. I did have rheumatoid arthritis, too. And all of that was accelerated by alcohol. And I wasn't doing anything about that yet.

My relationship with my new boss at Johns Hopkins was deteriorating. Dr. Bordley, who had hired me, had retired and been replaced by Dr. Nager, who I didn't like. I especially didn't like him when he asked me if I was looking for another job. I wrote myself a prescription for Antabuse to try to make me stop drinking. That didn't stop anything. When my body got swollen all over like a puffer fish, from drinking while taking Antabuse, I thought I would have to be hospitalized, but managed to avoid it.

One day, not long after my mom committed suicide, I got to work and found a booklet on my desk. It was from Blue Cross Blue Shield. It had 20 questions to answer about alcoholism. I read it over and, yes, I passed the test with flying colors. I didn't go right to the phone to call Alcoholics Anonymous. I tried to control it for a while longer. I didn't know, and still don't know, who placed the booklet there. I wouldn't go to a psychiatrist, because I was afraid I would lose my job.

Let's face it, I was losing my job.

CHAPTER 5

THE LAST PARTY

When the kids were ten, eight, and six, I decided to take a two-week vacation. I loaded the boys into the car and drove the 1200 miles from Maryland to my home farm in Michigan. Dad, Uncle Tom, and Aunt Ruth were going to keep the boys for me while I took some time off. I slept at the farm one night, turned around, and drove back to Maryland on black coffee and a prayer.

When I got home, I couldn't find Ross at first. It turned out that he was at a party at his secretary's house. Word was, they'd had a contest to see who could swim underwater the longest. Ross won that one–the only problem was that he didn't come up until people pulled him out of the pool. When I found out, I started crying and hollered at him, "What were you doing?" He said, "Well, I have to have a little fun sometime."

On June 20th there was a party to say goodbye to the

doctors leaving Hopkins and to welcome the new ones coming in on July first. I was on vacation, so why did I go? I guess it was the same thinking as Ross' by the pool: *I have to have a little fun sometimes.*

I went to the party at work, and the next morning Ross recounted how I'd behaved. It wasn't pretty. "Ross, I can't live one more day like this. I'm going to call AA." I meant Alcoholics Anonymous, but I had no idea what that would mean. He was getting ready for work and said, "Now don't go public with this. We've always been able to solve our problems together. It will be ok. You really aren't drinking as much as you used to. Some people, like my parents, would be uncomfortable if you didn't drink."

Oh my, I was beginning to wake up more. Ross had no idea how much I was drinking, and I wasn't about to go into the details with him. I really felt like hell. When Ross was at work that morning I called AA. A woman named Mary answered. "Hi," I said, "I'm Margaret and I think I have a drinking problem." I was waiting for her to ask me about my husband, my job and family. I figured I was just in a bad situation that would blow over.

Mary didn't ask me anything except, "Do you have any alcohol in the house?"

"Well, yes, right beside me here is half a gallon of Jim Beam."

"Ok," said Mary. "Dump it down the sink."

I looked at the bottle. The morning sun shining through

the bottle made the whiskey a beautiful color. I said, "You mean dump it now, while you're on the phone?"

"Yes, I'll wait. You don't have to drink it."

That was news to me. I didn't have to drink it. Amazing. I didn't have to drink it.

I dumped it out. I can still hear the *glug, glug, glug* as all that whiskey swirled down the drain.

Mary then told me that there was a meeting in College Park that night and that she would come by to pick me up. I told her I would get there on my own. I didn't want the neighbors to see her, to see an alcoholic coming over to our house. Mary asked if I could manage today without a drink. I said I would, that I was on vacation and had a week to go before I had to be back at work. I wanted to use this time to get well.

The AA meeting was at 8 p.m., and I discovered that the College Park meeting was a good place for me. It was far enough from home that I was sure there would be no one there that Ross or I knew. It felt safe to go there. Even so, I was terrified as I drove by the church. I saw people outside smoking, sitting on the steps, laughing in their light summer shirts. I drove by a couple more times, and more people were gathering and laughing. I parked and sat in the car. I didn't know where I was going or what I was doing. It felt just like going to California and leaving my life behind. I felt like I was in a free fall off the edge of a cliff, diving into...

I walked in.

Mary and Fern were at the door waiting for me. I didn't know Fern, but I fell into her loving arms. It was like heaven, like mother, like the unconditional love I'd never known. "Oh, honey," Fern said, "It's ok. We love you because you are an alcoholic, just like us. You will be fine. You don't have to drink. Just ask for help and, if it works, give thanks at night. Try it. You'll like it."

I went in to the beginner's meeting, in the back room, and cried the whole hour. The guy leading the meeting had been through hell. He had a big scar across his forehead and had been through much more than I had, but he was laughing and joking and happy. Something was working here. I felt curious. How could this happen?

Fern said not to talk to any men at the meeting, for now, and to leave my job, my degrees, and everything else at the door when I came in. She told me to be honest at all times, to not be mean, to not hurt myself or others, to get myself to meetings and listen, and I might find something I could learn. She also warned me that doctors and nurses often didn't do well in AA because they thought they knew it all.

Fern and I became close friends. I trusted her because she was a street survivor. She knew all about life. She sponsored and coached everyone, including men, women, and their families. When she didn't know how to help, she referred people to those who did. It was like I had entered into a living network that kept picking people up along the way and helping them.

The day after that first AA meeting, my head was clearing, I didn't have the shakes or a headache, and there was a glimmer of hope and peace. I had time for myself, the boys were doing well on the farm, and Ross was at work. This felt like a step in the right direction. I was caring for myself, and my body was responding. I was happier.

That first week, I went to a meeting every night, getting a lot in so I could do ok at work the next week. One night that week, Ross came home from work and said our lives had turned around 180 degrees overnight. He said he no longer had to worry that I would be killed in a car accident or never make it home. We were both calmer. I wanted him to come to AA too (though he never drank hard liquor, I felt sure he could learn something about himself, as I was beginning to), but that was where he drew the line. He said, "You are free to do what you need to do, and I am very happy about that, but I will take care of myself. We can work out the rest between us."

He was right, Shana. It's been 44 years since that conversation, and although Ross did go to a few open meetings, we tried to work out all the rest of it between us. After 58 years together, our love and understanding is deeper and more compassionate than ever before. I never found out who placed that booklet on my desk, but whoever they are, I owe them my life.

THAT TWO-WEEK vacation I took when I started going to the AA meetings came to an end, and Ross and I drove to the farm in Michigan to pick up our sons. They were happy that I was getting well.

I went back to work the next week and met with my boss, Dr. Nager. I told him that I knew our working relationship was not on track, for either of us, but that I was changing and I wanted to know what I could do for him. He seemed to be ready for me to say exactly that, because he had everything on the tip of his tongue for that meeting. He told me about rumors he'd heard, about things I'd said, and about other things that bothered him. I told him that, yes, I had said unkind things. I owned up to what was true about what he was saying, and I also let him know what was not true. I asked if I could meet with him weekly, so that we could always be connected to each other's ideas and actions, and so we could learn how we could help each other run the department. I told him that he was very important to me and to the institution. In addition, I told him that my sons were very important to me and I felt that I needed to be with them more. Therefore, I would no longer be able to attend Friday evening staff meetings. I would work hard during the week, but I wanted to be home by five or six on Fridays and have the weekends off.

Dr. Nager and I eventually became close friends and working partners on resolving many difficult surgical and staffing problems. I stayed on at Johns Hopkins for several more years, until my sons became teenagers. I could no longer hire more babysitters to solve the problems that my sons were facing, as they, too, were growing up. Johns Hopkins had a hospital and practice in Columbia, Maryland, which was only 15 minutes from home, instead of an hour and 15 minutes. I went to work there, where I was Chief of Otolaryngology/Head and Neck Surgery for the next twenty years.

MY RELATIONSHIPS with my patients changed after I stopped drinking, too. I was no longer in a hurry to be somewhere else, to get away from their suffering–or from my own. We had compassion for each other. I learned much from my patients, as they set examples for me about how to live, how to solve life problems, and how to die. We did it openly, together, with much love.

Surgery became only a very small aspect of caring for each patient, only a part of treating the whole person. Though I was trained to work on a small part of the body, people began coming to me for everything. Doctors referred their most difficult patients to me. If they didn't know what to do, they'd send them to Maggie. My practice became a form of *the buck stops here*. I saw and treated many people who had seen everyone else already—neurologists, psychiatrists, oral surgeons, cardiologists—you name the specialty. They had done every test and still had no answers.

I had time. I could listen. Most often, the patients themselves told me what was wrong with them. I would review all their tests and the studies that had been done with them, and they understood more about their own body and how it worked, and we found a way together. They learned how to manage life well with less suffering.

Performing surgery became easier. I was in charge, I was not in a hurry, I was no longer pushy, so surgery became more creative and effortless. I helped patients by following the laws of nature and finding ways they could maintain function as much as possible. The operating room was still a sanctuary for me. I give thanks to the human body for its amazing wish to live and heal, and to all those people who trusted me with their lives.

FOR A WHILE after I first stopped drinking, John would sniff my coffee mug to see what I was drinking, but then he stopped, because he came to trust that I wouldn't start drinking again. I told our sons about AA, and they came to some meetings. Then it was life as usual, or rather the usual I'd always wanted.

One day, John was chasing Jim around the house. I caught Jim and stopped him because he was hollering. He asked, "Mom, you going to a meeting tonight? I hope you remember what they say!" He knew I was getting better and he wanted me to keep at it. We were coming together as a family, coming to understand each other better, and I was getting well.

Alcoholism is no longer an issue for me. It's been 44 years since that last party. I still go to AA meetings, to a woman's meeting that's more of an empowerment and coaching session than anything else. Fern died four years ago, in a nursing home in Pennsylvania. She was coaching all the residents who lived there—always solving problems, like working out whose plants got to be in the sunny window, and advising about anything else that came up. I was with her in her last week. Her room was spare, but her mind was full. All earthly encumbrances were gone. A bouquet of daffodils and a glass for water sat at her bedside. She died of pancreatic cancer. She said she could feel it, but she wasn't interested in pain medication. She gave thanks and love.

My rheumatoid arthritis got worse. One Christmas, I took two weeks off work because I was having trouble walking and was feeling pain throughout my body. Ross carried me in to the doctor's office. The doctor gave me a couple of shots of cortisone and said, "There is nothing more I can do. You have arthritis." I started crying and asked him if he thought I should quit my job. He started to cry too. "I can't answer that," he said.

I did not improve over the next few days, and I started to worry about going back to work. I called Fern and told her I thought I was coming to the end and that nothing was working, I couldn't walk. She said, "Honey, I have seen you go through many of these arthritis cycles. You always get better. I think you'll make it through this one too." As she spoke those words I immediately felt the swelling in my body start to move. It was truth. It was hope. I went to the pool and I started to move again.

For a while I used a wheelchair for longer trips to the grocery store or art galleries, and I continued to work. Thirty years ago, I finally had a hip replacement, after finding a surgeon I could trust. Back then, joint replacements weren't as successful or common as they are today. By the time I had the hip surgery, after 30 years on steroids (prednisone), my bones were leeched of calcium. After the surgery, I fell often, and fractures were common–ankle, metatarsals, ribs, shoulder, wrist, humerus, all on separate falls.

When I fell and broke my neck, I finally woke up.

The message was this: *Slow down!*

I've learned to listen to my body and to stop dragging it around. I recommend avoiding surgery and prednisone when more conservative treatments work. Frozen joints in my spine, shoulders, elbows, feet, and ankles greatly limit the power and functioning of my body.

Doing Feldenkrais treatments for over four years has taught me how to achieve quite good mobility in spite of the challenges. Feldenkrais gave me a simple process: start like a baby, remembering what it was like to just roll on the floor. Stop causing the pain. Any pain, not just body pain.

Working and doing things in spite of pain causes the body to resist, thereby becoming stiffer and more easily damaged. Become more aware of body alignment. Moving a body while bent over and stiff is worse than driving a car with a flat tire. Don't try to fix all pain. It passes. It heals itself with alignment and rest. Treat your body with love and kindness. Even imaginary movement is healing.

All of that was hard-won wisdom for me.

Today, I walk almost two miles every day and swim a couple times each week. I take time to realign my body on the floor, too, especially if I notice pain in my feet or neck or when any area starts to hurt.

As for my mind, the depression is gone. Sometimes I'm sad or down for minutes or maybe an hour, and this is good. It reminds me that my thinking is off. And now when that happens, I stop and pay attention. I went to a 10-day Vipassana meditation retreat that was life-changing. I don't react to everything. I laugh more and I am happy. My mind no longer runs the show. With meditation, I am in touch with universal inner wisdom and love–my connection to all beings.

In writing this, I have discovered how similar, even identical, my mom and I were and are—the postpartum depression, the sadness, the insanity, rheumatoid arthritis—all common things, and all lessons. I am still my mother's daughter.

And I am home.

EPILOGUE

By Shana Fletcher

In my life, I admire all of the people who are closest to me. I have strong passion for all of my family members and friends who believe in me and love me. But there is an outstanding person in my family that I would like to use as an example of someone in my life whose philosophy I agree with and am inspired by, and who I aspire to be like. This is my grandmother. Her name is Margaret Mackrain Fletcher.

She is my soulmate, one of my best friends, and the first person I call when I'm having strong emotional feelings or troubles. What I admire most about my grandmother is how strong she is. How free, liberated, intelligent, and extraordinary she is. She grew up on a farm in cold Upper Michigan, the oldest of 7 children. Her mother battled depression, and eventually my grandma had to raise all of her younger siblings because of this, until she left at the age of 16, to go to board a train and head to California and start her own life. From that point on, she went from having no money to going to the University of Michigan, shocking the world that she was one of the only female medical students at the time, and becoming a well-known otolaryngologist (ear, nose, and throat doctor). She even did surgery on Chiang Kaishek's wife! After a couple decades of doing surgery, she fell ill with rheumatoid arthritis.

Eventually, this would end her career and put her in extreme physical and emotional pain for the rest of her life. Every day, she thinks about life, her luck, and how to make life even better, more everyday. What inspires me is the pain that she goes through and the way she battles it. Even though she is not religious, she uses a lot of the same teachings of many different religions, especially the Asian ones when it comes to her life. She is very spiritual, believes in meditation, but especially writing. Depression runs in our family, and unfortunately I have acquired it myself. It is a gene, and there is no way to be rid of it. But Grandma has taught me to not be afraid. Ever since I could talk, I feared many things, unusual things. My Grandma taught me to breathe and write my feelings, and to tell myself that these scary thoughts are not true. Today, I still have similar feelings of fear, but more within myself. I sometimes fear that I am a bad person, and that I will lose all of my loved ones because I'm not good enough. But because I have my grandmother and her beautiful mind, we help each other fight these feelings everyday. I am not the only one she's inspired. Everyone who has at least a conversation with her will tell me how amazing they think she is. How intelligent, out of this world. She is one of the main leaders of AA and she Skypes with women across the world, every week, to inspire them, just like she's inspired me. I am beyond lucky to have her as my teacher and my idol and my blood.

I agree with Confucius' teachings, that "anyone can become a morally upright and righteous individual." And that "it takes a lifetime filled with hard work and effort to make yourself a truly moral and righteous individual." I believe that consciousness of life and our earth is the most important way of being a human being. To think about our lives on this earth and in this universe, but stop thinking about our small lives in our specific places, is strong for a human. Because I believe that we are on this earth, and we should think about this world that we may be only seeing for a certain amount of time. To meditate. To live with peace in our life and to aspire to be happy, every day, and not rot on this beautiful planet. I believe that anyone with these thoughts, or thoughts about living in peace and being inspired to be happy, and who teaches other people about their feelings, is a truly admirable human being.

September 18, 2014

ACKNOWLEDGMENTS

I am grateful for my parents and family, who provided what I needed as a child: a strong work ethic, and the fearlessness and strength to face what life offers. I would like to acknowledge the enormous help given to me by Angela Lauria, president of The Author Incubator. Without her help, this book would not have been written. Thank you to my patient editor, Grace Kerina, for her competence and wisdom. I wish to thank Ross Fletcher, my love and partner of nearly six decades, for his unending support every step of the way. Also, thanks to our three sons, John, Jim, and David, and to our grandchildren, Ana and John Fletcher. It was great trying to stay one step ahead of them when they were growing up. Now they're taking us into their jobs and lives and are many laps ahead. Thanks to Robin Levien and Arlene Bradley, my friends and partners on this spiritual journey. Great thanks to the Universe for creating amazing human bodies that want to live, to love, and to heal.

ABOUT THE AUTHOR

Dr. Margaret Fletcher is a retired otolaryngology/head and neck surgeon.

After training at the University of Michigan, she had appointments on the faculties of the University of Maryland and Johns Hopkins. For the last 20 years of her medical practice, she was Chief of Otolaryngology/Head and Neck Surgery at the Columbia Medical Plan in Columbia, Maryland. She lives with her husband in Ashton, Maryland.

Since her retirement, Margaret has continued to study the art and science of human healing. She helps elderly people, family, and friends with their aging and end-of-life care. She also contributes to the care of veterans and provides scholarships for students in need. She has had great joy caring for her granddaughter when her actor son is working in venues outside of New York.

ABOUT DIFFERENCE PRESS

Difference Press offers solopreneurs, including life coaches, healers, consultants, and community leaders, a comprehensive solution to get their books written, published, and promoted. A boutique-style alternative to self-publishing, Difference Press boasts a fair and easy-to-understand profit structure, low-priced author copies, and author-friendly contract terms. Its founder, Dr. Angela Lauria, has been bringing to life the literary ventures of hundreds of authors -in-transformation since 1994.

YOUR DELICIOUS BOOK

Your Delicious Book is a trailblazing program for aspiring authors who want to create a non-fiction book that becomes a platform for growing their business or communicating their message to the world in a way that creates a difference in the lives of others.

In a market where hundreds of thousands books are published every year and never heard from again, all of The Author Incubator participants have bestsellers that are actively changing lives and making a difference. The program, supported by quarterly Difference Press book-marketing summits, has a proven track record of helping aspiring authors write books that matter. Our team will hold your hand from idea to impact, showing you how to write a book, what elements must be present in your book for it to deliver the results you need, and how to meet the needs of your readers. We give you all the editing, design, and technical support you need to ensure a high-quality book published to the Kindle platform. Plus, authors in the program are connected to a powerful community of authors-in-transformation and published bestselling authors.

TACKLING THE TECHNICAL ASPECTS OF PUBLISHING

The comprehensive coaching, editing, design, publishing, and marketing services offered by Difference Press mean that your book will be edited by a pro, designed by an experienced graphic artist, and published digitally and in print by publishing industry experts. We handle all of the technical aspects of your book's creation so you can spend more of your time focusing on your business.

APPLY TO WRITE WITH US

To submit an application to our acquisitions team visit www.YourDeliciousBook.com.

OTHER BOOKS BY DIFFERENCE PRESS

Confessions of an Unlikely Runner: A Guide to Racing and Obstacle Courses for the Averagely Fit and Halfway Dedicated

by Dana L. Ayers

Matter: How to Find Meaningful Work That's Right for You and Your Family

by Caroline Greene

Reclaiming Wholeness: Letting Your Light Shine Even If You're Scared to Be Seen

by Kimberlie Chenoweth

The Well-Crafted Mom: How to Make Time for Yourself and Your Creativity within the Midst of Motherhood

by Kathleen Harper

Lifestyle Design for a Champagne Life: Find Out Why the Law of Attraction Isn't Working, Learn the Secret to Lifestyle Design, and Create Your Champagne Life

by Cassie Parks

No More Drama: How to Make Peace with Your Defiant Kid

by Lisa Cavallaro

The Nurse Practitioner's Bag: Become a Healer, Make a Difference, and Create the Career of Your Dreams

by Nancy Brook

Farm Girl Leaves Home: An American Narrative of Inspiration and Transformation

by Margaret Fletcher

Whoops! I Forgot to Achieve My Potential

by Maggie Huffman

Only 10s: Using Distraction to Get the Right Things Done

by Mark Silverman

The Inside Guide to MS: How to Survive a New Diagnosis When Your Whole Life Changes (And You Just Want to Go Home)

by Andrea Hanson

Lee & Me: What I Learned from Parenting a Child with Adverse Childhood Experiences

by Wendy Gauntner

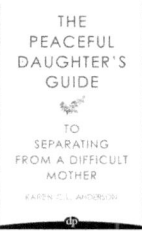

The Peaceful Daughter's Guide to Separating from A Difficult Mother: Freeing Yourself From The Guilt, Anger, Resentment and Bitterness

by Karen C. L. Anderson

Soulful Truth Telling: Disbelieving the Lies That Keep Us From the Love We Desire

by Sharon Pope

Personal Finance That Doesn't Suck: A 5-step Guide to Quit Budgeting, Start Wealth Building and Get the Most from Your Money

by Mindy Crary

The Cancer Whisperer: How to Let Cancer Heal Your Life

by Sophie Sabbage

www.ingramcontent.com/pod-product-compliance
Lightning Source LLC
LaVergne TN
LVHW020937090426
835512LV00020B/3399